BATH TO EVERCREECH JUNCTION

Vic Mitchell and Keith Smith

MP Middleton Press

INTRODUCTION

This album is the second in our trilogy centred on the hub of the old Somerset & Dorset Railway empire at Evercreech Junction. As in our other books, we have included full size reproductions of the Ordnance Survey 25" to 1 mile maps to show the railway and its environment. Most of the photographs have not appeared in books before, as we have selected them from less commonly used sources but some may appear familiar, having been taken from the popular vantage points.

Cover picture: One of the popular ex-LMS class 2P 4-4-0s waits in one of the centre roads at Bath Green Park in 1954. The massive roof now echoes to the rattle of supermarket trolleys instead of the music of the majestic machines of the steam era. (F.W.Ivey)

First published November 1988
Revised and reprinted January 1992

ISBN 0 906520 60 6

© *Middleton Press 1988*

Design - Deborah Goodridge

Typeset by CitySet - Bosham 573270

Published by Middleton Press
            Easebourne Lane
            Midhurst
            West Sussex
            GU29 9AZ
            Tel: (0730) 813169

Printed & bound by Biddles Ltd,
            Guildford and Kings Lynn

CONTENTS

MAPS

The 1956 map shows the Western Region routes with a narrow line and those used by Southern Region trains with a wide line.

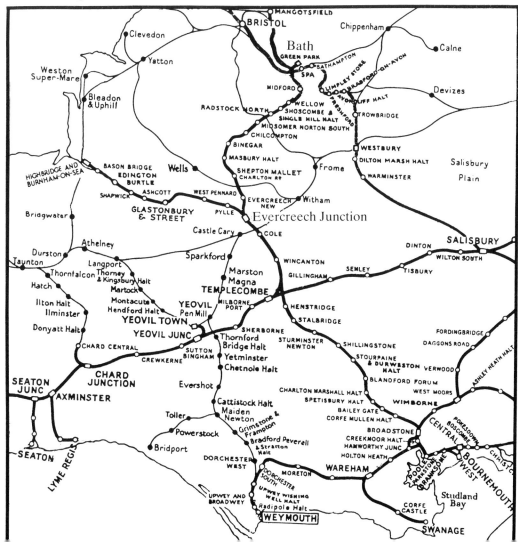

GEOGRAPHICAL SETTING

Bath is situated in the Avon Gap in the southern extension of the Cotswolds and to take the line south, two tunnels were necessary to penetrate this limestone mass and reach the steep-sided valley of the Midford Brook. This is a tributary of the River Avon, which continues south as the Wellow Brook to Radstock, the railway running roughly parallel to it.

At Radstock, the line begins a seven mile climb onto the plateau of the Mendips. Coal measures have until recently been an important aspect of the economic geology of the Radstock area. Further south, limestone has been the main mineral of commercial interest, used for roadstone, building purposes and lime production. Igneous activity has created mineralisation with veins, rich in compounds of zinc and iron.

Evercreech is at the northern border of the more level part of Somerset, this area being one of productive agricultural land, particularly in respect of dairy products.

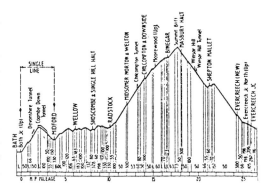

PASSENGER SERVICES

The initial service was one of four trains each way, weekdays only. (Sunday trains were never operated regularly, apart from some excursions to Bournemouth between the wars.) Frequency increased slowly – six by 1884 and by 1890 there were five stopping trains plus three expresses, these carrying through coaches to and from the North. Through trains commenced in 1910 and, by 1914, the S&D route was at its zenith with seven expresses and five slow trains.

World War I resulted in all but one fast service being withdrawn but recovery followed, there being five expresses and eight stoppers in 1924. 1927 saw the name "Pines Express" applied to the Bournemouth - Manchester service. This ran throughout the year, complete with dining car, until 1962, except between 1939 - 49.

World War II brought a curtailed service of four stopping trains initially, but by 1942 the timetable had improved slightly with five slows and one fast available.

The post-war upsurge in holiday traffic had a dramatic effect on traffic, particularly on summer Saturdays. In the mid-1950s, there were up to 12 expresses on these days in addition to the local trains.

As the effect of increased private motoring reduced passenger demand in the early 1960s, through trains from the North, were withdrawn in September 1962. Thereafter, there were ten departures from Bath, three of which started at Bristol. The 4.20pm only stopped at Shepton Mallet and the 6.05pm terminated at Binegar, but did not run on Saturdays.

Postponement of closure from 3rd January to 6th March 1966 resulted in a temporary timetable of four stopping trains, all terminating at Templecombe.

Up departures at intermediate stations

	1910	1924	1938	1948	1965	1966
Evercreech New	6	8	7	5	6	4
Shepton Mallet	10	11	11	8	8	4
Masbury	4	5	6	3	1	1
Binegar	6	7	6	4	6	3
Chilcompton	5	8	7	6	6	3
Midsomer Norton	7	8	9	7	9	4
Radstock	8	9	9	7	9	4
Shoscombe	–	–	6	5	8	4
Wellow	5	6	6	5	7	3
Midford	5	6	6	4	7	3

(This table excludes trains operating less than five days per week and those stopping by request for journeys in one or other direction.)

HISTORICAL BACKGROUND

The first public railway in the area was the Great Western Railway's Bristol to Bath line, which opened on 31st August 1840. An earlier railway to Bath was built in 1755 and was used for the carriage of building stone from Combe Down.

The next line in the district was a broad gauge branch from the GWR main line at Frome to the coal mining town of Radstock and this came into use for freight only on 14th November 1854. In the same year, the Somerset Central Railway was opened between Highbridge and Glastonbury, it being extended to Templecombe on 3rd February 1862. In 1863, the SCR was amalgamated with the Dorset Central Railway, with the object of linking the Bristol and English Channels by rail. This proved to be a financial disaster and by 1866, the Somerset & Dorset Railway was bankrupt.

The Midland Railway reached Bath in 1869 and it was to this company that the ailing S&DR turned when seeking a terminus for its northern extension. This line, from Evercreech Junction, was opened on 20th July 1874 and was built (for six miles) on the course of the Somerset Coal Canal. This canal was opened north from Radstock in 1804 to the River Avon but a flight of nineteen locks above Midford was never completed. A 3′5½″ gauge tramway was substituted here, and in 1815 this was extended south along the towpath of the canal, which then became redundant.

A line from Bristol to Radstock was opened on 3rd September 1873 and subsequently operated by the GWR who completed conversion of their line to Frome from broad to standard gauge on 25th June 1874. Passenger services between Frome and Radstock commenced on 5th July 1875. Thus the railway facilities at Radstock changed dramatically in less than two years.

The Bath extension of the SDR was the company's last hope for survival as it expected that a link between the Midlands and the South Coast, traversing the Somerset coalfield, would be very profitable. Although this extension was built in a mere two years (despite the need to construct eleven viaducts and four tunnels), the company was financially exhausted. On 1st November 1875, an agreement was signed whereby the Midland Railway and the London & South Western Railway would jointly lease the S&DR, and thus the Somerset & Dorset Joint Railway was born. The lessees each foresaw the opportunity to develop traffic between their respective railways and this certainly happened. The LSWR took responsibility for civil engineering and signalling and the MR undertook the management of rolling stock. The Joint Committee eventually located the traffic manager at Bath.

Doubling of the track took place in stages but the northern four miles remained single, owing to the expense of duplicating the two long tunnels.

Midford	– Wellow	28 August 1892
Wellow	– Radstock	1 July 1894
Radstock	– Binegar	circa 1886
Binegar	– Shepton Mallet	20 November 1892
Shepton Mallet	– Evercreech New	5 February 1888
Evercreech New	– Evercreech Jnc.	28 August 1886

Further competition from the GWR came when new lines crossed the S&D route at Shepton Mallet in 1878 and at Midford in 1910. The grouping of the railways resulted in the S&DJR becoming jointly vested in the SR and LMS in 1923, although still managed by a joint committee. On 1st January 1930, reorganisation resulted in the LMS being in control of operating, traffic and commercial staff and the much admired Prussian blue livery disappeared. The SR undertook all maintenance of fixed equipment and accounting.

The formation of British Railways in 1948 resulted in the London Midland Region operating the line from offices in Bath while the Southern Region supervised traffic from Southampton. The line became "nobody's baby" and was thrust upon the Western Region in 1950. After struggling for survival, a lingering death ensued. Through freight trains were withdrawn in 1959 and through passenger services to the North ceased in 1962. Most local goods facilities were closed in 1963 - 64 and the residual passenger trains were curtailed on 7th March 1966, after vociferous protests and several postponements.

BATH GREEN PARK

The hot springs attracted the Romans, but after their influence ceased, twelve centuries passed before the town began to develop as a health resort. Before the arrival of the railways the city had expanded and been laid out with fine squares and elegant crescents. An historic abbey and fine architecture added to the attraction of the well situated centre which, by the end of the century, had over 50,000 inhabitants.

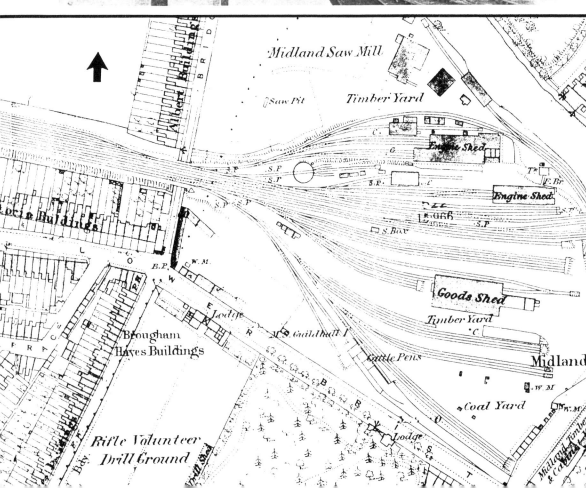

1. The station began to receive MR trains from Bristol on 4th August 1869, although the steel framed train shed was not complete. Recent research has show that reports of a temporary station west of the river were untrue. "Green Park" was added to the station name on 18th June 1951, to replace the unofficial "Queen Square". (Lens of Sutton)

2. As at Bournemouth Central, fully glazed end screens to the trains shed were provided but all glazing was lost during WWII, as were the former SDJR offices at 13-14 Green Park Buildings. The line was once noted for its locomotive cleanliness, as illustrated by this Derby-built example. (Lens of Sutton)

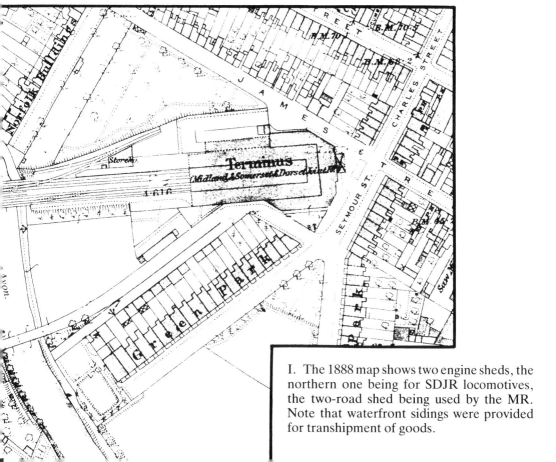

I. The 1888 map shows two engine sheds, the northern one being for SDJR locomotives, the two-road shed being used by the MR. Note that waterfront sidings were provided for transhipment of goods.

3. A photograph from August 1928, features SDJR no.44 reversing towards the locomotive depot after its train from the south had departed. GR on the bonded warehouse refers to the King. It was used for the storage of duty free spirits and its cellars extended a great distance under the platforms. (K. Nunn/LCGB)

4. In 1938, improvements were made to the station environment – even the paintwork appears clean, a feature few can remember. The concourse and platforms were boarded, so that the movement of every passenger and barrow would be heard anywhere in the station. (L. Maggs)

5. By the time the classical frontage was photographed in 1948, it had suffered years of neglect and the mellow Bath stone had become soot encrusted. Beyond the cobbled forecourt, the canopy has become almost invisible with grime. (D. Cullum collection)

6. Passengers were often required to walk beyond the boarded section of platform 2 to reach their train if it was a short one. This meant that it could be kept clear of the engine release crossover. The small kiosk, seen on platform 1 on 19th July 1958, was intended to compensate for the lack of refreshment facilities on most through trains reversing at this station. (S.W. Baker)

7. Glass was not replaced until long after trains ceased to run and so coaches and vans stabled in the centre roads remained unprotected. Class 2P no.40698 waits to depart with the 1.10pm stopping train to Templecombe on 22nd July 1958, two months after the station had been transferred to the Western Region. (R.C. Riley)

8. The 12.20pm Bournemouth West to Nottingham awaits reversal on 24th June 1961, having been hauled by no.34041 *Wilton* and piloted from Evercreech Junction by class 2P no.40697. The sign is pointing to the main refreshment room, which was at the east end of platform 1. (J.J. Smith)

9. On 24th June 1961, the up "Pines Express" arrived behind class 2P no.40569 and 9F no.92000, but as there was no crossover at platform 1, they had to wait for the train to depart north before they could earn further revenue. The finger post boards can now be seen in the SDRT Museum at Washford station, on the West Somerset Railway. (J.J. Smith)

10. This 1963 photograph shows the rail access to the bonded store for sealed vans. After unloading, the barrels were moved on a narrow gauge railway in the cellars. The lamp post reminds us that the station was gas lit to the end. The shed was demolished in 1981 and one of the cast iron lattice windows was later incorporated into the new engine shed at Washford. (C.L. Caddy)

11. The last trains ran on 6th March 1966 and this is the scene four weeks later, as the buildings faced an uncertain future. In 1971, it was listed Grade 2 and soon purchased by the City Council, but it was not until 1979 that a restoration scheme was agreed. (C.L. Caddy)

Somerset & Dorset Rly.
Joint Committee.
MONTHLY RETURN
Evercreech Jn.
Bath
Evercreech Jc. to
BATH
Third Class. Fare 5/7
0964

12. Sainsbury's opened a supermarket on part of the site of the former goods yard in November 1982 and contributed substantially towards the £1.5M cost of the restoration of the station. The re-glazed roof now protects shoppers loading their cars with groceries and also provides an area for community activities, such as concerts and exhibitions. The station offices now serve a variety of retail and leisure uses. (S.W. Baker)

13. The classical facade has been magnificently restored – compare the newly turned balusters with the eroded ones in picture 11. The doorway on the left had previously served the parcels office, the area having earlier been the third class ladies waiting room. (S.W. Baker)

14. The timber-built SDJR locomotive shed is seen on 7th June 1930, with nos.320 and 326 (built at Derby for the SDJR) showing their differences in footplating and tenders. The roof span on the left covered the workshops but from 1930, the former MR shed was mainly used for repairs. The shear legs, on the left, were erected in 1878 and used for raising one end of a locomotive for wheel removal. (H.C. Casserley)

Green Park Station. Open 9.30 a.m. - 6.00 p.m. Tuesday: Crafts. Wednesday: Antiques and Collectables. Thursday: Art. Friday: Designer Market. Saturday: General.

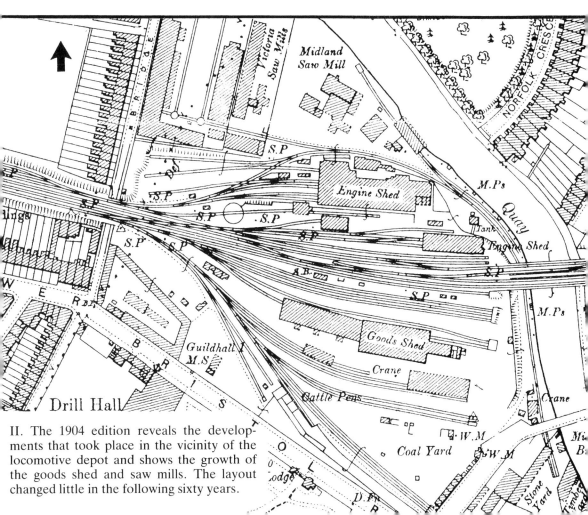

II. The 1904 edition reveals the developments that took place in the vicinity of the locomotive depot and shows the growth of the goods shed and saw mills. The layout changed little in the following sixty years.

15. The coaling stage was also made of timber but was rebuilt in brick in 1954. The steel coal tubs (right) were filled manually and pushed onto the platform projecting over the tender. The overhead conveyor was elec-trically operated and used mainly for moving bins of ash. It was severed prior to the coal stage rebuilding and never restored.
(H.C. Casserley)

❦

The MR shed was erected in 1869-70 and the SDR built theirs in 1874-75. This was doubled in width in 1878 to accommodate four roads and was increased in length in 1884.

16. This August 1928 view shows the conveyor passing over the ash wagon. Its intricate supports appear to be old roof trusses. On the left is the 1891 sand drying furnace, another requirement for considerable labour. No.64 was one of five 0–6–0s built at Derby in 1896 for the SDJR.
(K. Nunn/LCGB)

❦

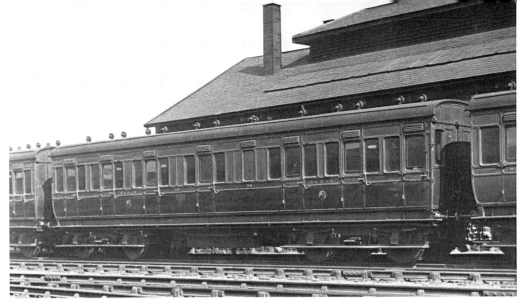

17. The MR shed ventilators are shown clearly in this 1930 view of SDJR coach no.36, which had 4½ third, 2 first and 1 lavatory compartment. The much admired blue livery can now only be seen in paintings. The coach was built at the S&DJR's Highbridge Works in 1900 and acquired its odd coupe compartment later, when an earlier luggage section was converted for passengers. (H.C. Casserley)

LAVATORY CARRIAGES OR SALOONS.

When ordinary carriages, having lavatory compartments, are attached to trains, the Station Master at the starting point will be held responsible for seeing that the lavatory is in proper working order, and the cistern filled with water; and when carriages of this description are attached to trains running a distance of 100 miles or upwards, the cisterns must, if necessary, be refilled with water at the intermediate stations at which the trains stop. When the lamps in the ordinary compartments are lighted, the lamps in the lavatory compartments must also be lighted.

18. On 3rd September 1949, the camera recorded the oil tanks erected as part of an oil firing programme and never used, owing to political indecision. In the background is sister engine, no.53800. These two class 7Fs were the first supplied to the SDJR (as nos.80 & 81) in 1914, and were then the most powerful locomotives on the line. (S.W. Baker)

19. The roof of Bath Station Signal Box is visible above the leading coach of the "Pines Express" on 22nd July 1958, as class 5 no.73028 departs for the North. Other features of note are the goods shed extension on the right, and the former MR stone-built locomotive shed, on the left. (R.C. Riley)

20. (Below) On the same day, no.53800 faces one of the short-armed ex-MR shunt signals, not found further south. Behind this engine is a class 2P, standing on the incline to the coal stage, while on the right, another takes water. (R.C. Riley)

21. (Lower right) On 20th November 1961, puddles added to the problems of shunting the curved sidings. On the right is the yard office and an ex-MR signal, and in the distance is the 10-ton crane and the main goods shed, which contained a number of 30cwt cranes. (P. Hay)

22. Sole access to a locomotive shed across a turntable was usually avoided, as its failure could trap a fleet of engines. However, the ex-MR shed was mainly used for repairs and the ex-SDJR one, on the left, used as a running shed. Class 4F no.44146 and class 5 no.44944 were both out of traffic on 14th July 1962. (E. Wilmshurst)

23. The prosperous MR built their shed of stone, with ornate cast iron windows, unlike their neighbour's cheap timber affair. Class 3F no.47506 stands over the pit and under the smoke hood on 18th September 1965. (A.G. Thorpe)

24. In 1934, a 60ft turntable was installed close to the ex-MR shed. The previous 46ft one (from 1878) had been shared by the MR and SDJR, its location being evident on the 1904 map. The loco crew apply their muscles to the gearing on 26th June 1962. These powerful (7F) freight engines were used on some summer passenger services, from 1950 onwards. (R.C. Riley)

25. On 2nd June 1963, the yard was sufficiently clear to record the trackwork details and the position of the ashpits. The ash wagon is on the right – finding sufficient labour for the unpleasant task of loading it was a problem for many shedmasters. The loss of the overhead conveyor was no doubt regretted by then. (C.L. Caddy)

26. Saturday 5th March 1966 was the last day of public services, this picture being the signalman's view of the uncontrollable trespass that day and of the grounded coach body, once used for enginemen's mutual improvement classes. Platform 2 accommodated eight coaches and no. 1, nine. The rear of the longer trains, particularly when doubleheaded, often spanned the River Avon and stood, as here, near the ex-MR shed. The goods depot remained in use until 31st May 1971.
(R.E.Ruffell)

III. The 1888 survey shows the position of the original signal boxes and the siding to Bath Gas Works. Hopmead was the name given to a siding opened on 30th April 1931 and used for petrol tankers. It branched from the up shunting line (which was on the down side for SDJR trains!), near Hopmead Buildings.

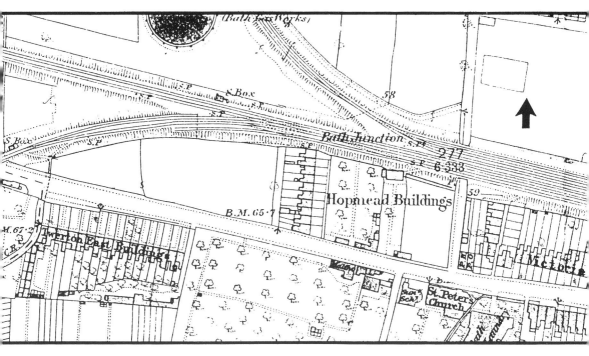

28. The Lower Bristol Road was crossed on a skew bridge (lower left on map), on a 1 in 50 gradient down to Bath. The bridge and the houses have now disappeared, only the nearby "Royal Oak" serving as a marker. A standard gauge electric tramway ran under this bridge from 1904 until 1939. (F.W. Ivey)

27. The view from the footplate of class 7F no.53810 on 26th June 1962 includes class 8F 2–8–0 no.48660, with a coal train from Midsomer Norton; Bath Junction Box and the double track to Mangotsfield and Bristol. The signal box came into use on 13th April 1924, replacing the MR box (north of the main line) and the SDJR one, which was near the brake van. (R.C. Riley)

SOUTH OF BATH

29. The next siding south was opened in 1913 to serve the coal depot and bakery of the Twerton Co-operative Society Ltd. It remained in use until 30th November 1967, more than a year after the line southwards had been totally closed. For many years, the banking engine left Bath at 7.25am to propel wagons into the siding. The hut housed a ground frame which was opened by an Annetts key attached to the banking engine staff. (C. Maggs)

IV. The 1904 edition has the GWR Bath - Bristol passing under the SDJR single line from which a siding runs into the brick and tile works, earlier known as May's. Rail traffic would comprise coal inwards and clay products outwards, traffic flowing between about 1890 and 1950.

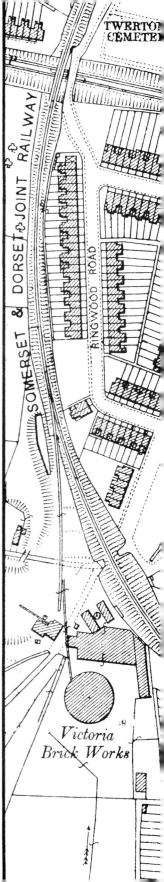

30. The 8.00am Crewe to Bournemouth West train is hauled up the two-mile climb, at mainly 1 in 50, towards the 440yd Devonshire Tunnel on 4th July 1959. A short level stretch was situated by the Co-op Bakery, visible above the third coach. Class 4F no.44523 pilots class 5 4–6–0 no.73028. (J.J. Smith)

31. After traversing a complete semi-circle, passengers had their last view of historic Bath as their train entered this cutting at the approach to Devonshire Tunnel. The train is the 7.00am Cleethorpes to Bournemouth West on 4th July 1959 and the locomotives are class 2P no.40564 and "West Country" no.34043 *Combe Martin*. (J.J. Smith)

32. Turning the camera 90°, one week later, class 7F no.53804 emerges from the tunnel with the 12 noon from Templecombe. Owing to financial constraints, the tunnels on the line were built to minimum dimensions and devoid of ventilation shafts. Even the portals were as plain as possible. (S.C. Nash)

33. After passing through Combe Down Tunnel, which was over a mile long and on a falling gradient for down trains, passengers soon found themselves enjoying the delightful scenery surrounding Tucking Mill Viaduct. Midford distant signal is seen behind the 10.38am Manchester to Bournemouth West, headed by class 4Fs nos.44422 and 44559 on 20th August 1955. William Smith, regarded as the "Father" of geology, lived below the viaduct for many years. (S.C. Nash)

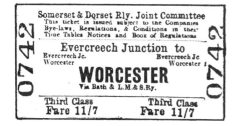

Somerset & Dorset Rly. Joint Committee
This ticket is issued subject to the Companies
Bye-laws, Regulations, & Conditions in their
Time Tables Notices and Book of Regulations

Evercreech Junction to
Evercreech Jc.   Evercreech Jc
Worcester   Worcester f

WORCESTER
Via Bath & L.M.& S.Ry.

Third Class   Third Class
Fare 11/7   Fare 11/7

0742

35. The goods yard points had been relaid with flat-bottom rail before being photographed on 11th August 1962. Class 4 2–6–0 no.76013 emerges from the Long Arch with the 1.08pm Bournemouth West to Bath, its smoke still lingering around the coaches. The yard closed on 10th June 1963, the rails being lifted twelve months later. (E. Wilmshurst)

MIDFORD

34. The goods yard and small shed were situated ¼ mile north of the station, as the line runs along the side of a steeply walled valley and level ground was not available any nearer. This 1963 view includes the ground frame box and the 6-ton capacity crane, near the gate. (C.L. Caddy)

36. A northward view shows Midford signal box, with pitched roof (centre) but does not include the Camerton branch, which opened in 1910. The signal box was partly demolished on 29th July 1936, when an engine (class 3F 0–6–0T no.7620) ran away unattended from Writhlington to the outskirts of Bath, propelling a decreasing number of wagons. (Dr. L.E. Smith/R.C. Riley collection)

Situated in a deep valley on the Bath-Frome road, the small community was devoid of an Anglican church and after 1815 became the transhipment point for coal from the tramway from Radstock to the Somerset Coal Canal. Three horses would haul about 10 tons of coal in eight tram tubs down the valley from Radstock and at Midford it would be transferred to barges for conveyance to towns, mainly on the Kennet & Avon and Wilts & Berks Canals.

37. Looking west, the Camerton line is on the embankment in the foreground and the road to Bath is seen climbing on the left. Midford station is partly obscured by trees. (Dr. L.E. Smith/R.C. Riley)

38. Looking north from the signal box in June 1963, it is clear that the line was built on a shelf on the hillside. Beyond the backing signal, steps were provided up the rock face to give more direct access to the upper part of the village. (C.L. Caddy)

39. The lamp, apparently without post, illuminated the footpath. The wrong road or backing signal could be used for up goods trains that needed to set back to make another attempt to climb the incline to Combe Down Tunnel. Less obvious is the 35mph speed restriction sign, in need of some fresh white paint. (E. Wilmshurst)

40. Only the embankment of the Camerton branch remained, when this photograph was taken on 10th July 1960, the branch having last been used in 1952 for the filming of the "Titfield Thunderbolt". Class 7F no.53809 heads north with empty stock from Bournemouth to Derby. (R.C. Riley)

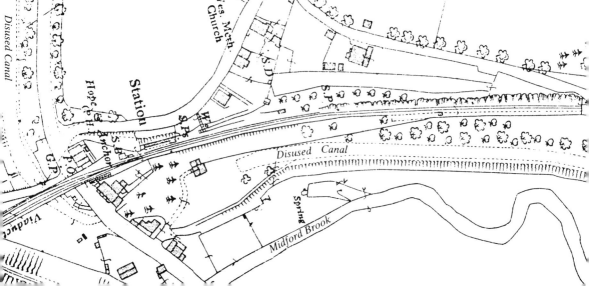

41. An up local train leaves the northern limit of double track on 7th August 1965 and approaches the unique replacement signal box with its flat roof, boarded sides, brick back and stone base. On the right is the last arch of the GWR viaduct – a steel girder bridge once spanned the lane and linked it with the embankment seen in the previous picture. Until about 1959, an additional siding was available on the up side, in the distance. (S.W. Baker)

V. The 1932 map reveals that the weighing machine (W.M.) was situated in the highway, from which the yard had two gateways. The dotted lines indicate the position of part of the former Somerset Coal Canal. A portion of the GWR Camerton branch is shown in the lower left corner.

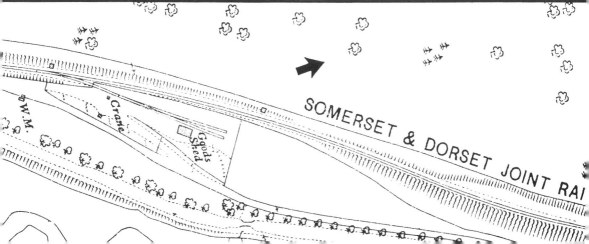

WELLOW

Bell's Guide of 1929 described the village as "picturesquely situated on the north slope of the valley and is reached by *steep and narrow roads which demand very careful driving*. Though the place is remote and difficult of access, except by rail, it deserves a visit." The charming limestone dwellings housed 1100 people when the railway arrived, the figure increasing to 1500 by the turn of the century. There was considerable industry with a water-powered corn mill and watercress beds in the valley, and a large forge, maltings and steam mills in the village. The latter ground fuller's earth, then used mainly in the treatment of wool and now in great demand by the chemical industry and producers of cat litter.

42. The grey limestone building was typical of those at the other stations southwards, although bricks were commonly used for the chimneys. The staff demonstrate their skill in spinning milk churns while the background shows that the valley side is slightly less steeply sloping than at Midford.
(Lens of Sutton)

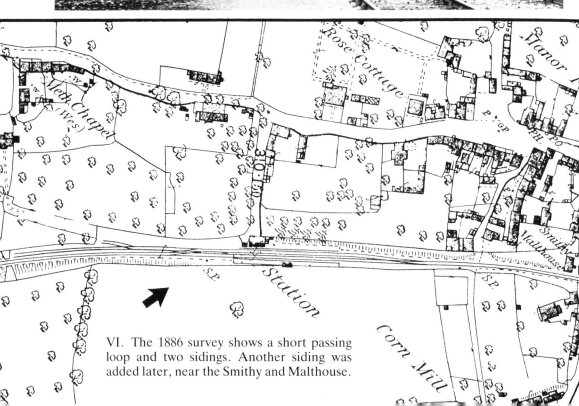

VI. The 1886 survey shows a short passing loop and two sidings. Another siding was added later, near the Smithy and Malthouse.

43. The bay window was on the station master's office and the large chimney in the distance was on a forge, which produced agricultural equipment on a scale greater than most village smithies. Nearby were steam mills processing locally quarried fuller's earth, these businesses justifying provision of the siding seen in the distance. It was not used after 1912. (Lens of Sutton)

44. 0–4–4T no.1387, designed by Johnson in 1881, runs in with an up stopping train, the small goods yard being just visible in the distance. The gentlemen's toilet was discreetly placed on the end of most stations but is prominent in this photograph, which was taken on 21st September 1936.
(H.C. Casserley)

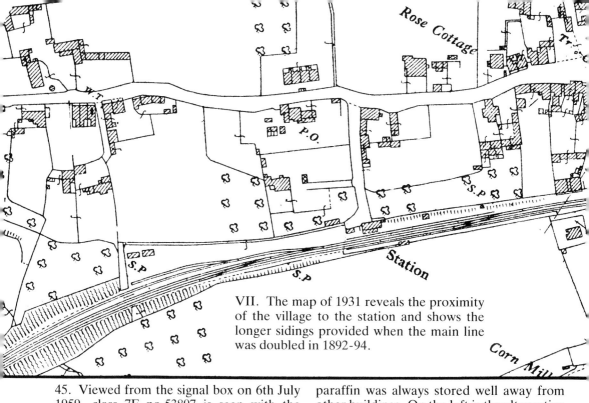

VII. The map of 1931 reveals the proximity of the village to the station and shows the longer sidings provided when the main line was doubled in 1892-94.

45. Viewed from the signal box on 6th July 1959, class 7F no.53807 is seen with the 6.05am from Templecombe. The iron hut, by the fourth wagon, was the lamp room – the paraffin was always stored well away from other buildings. On the left is the alternative passenger access to the down platform. (R.C. Riley)

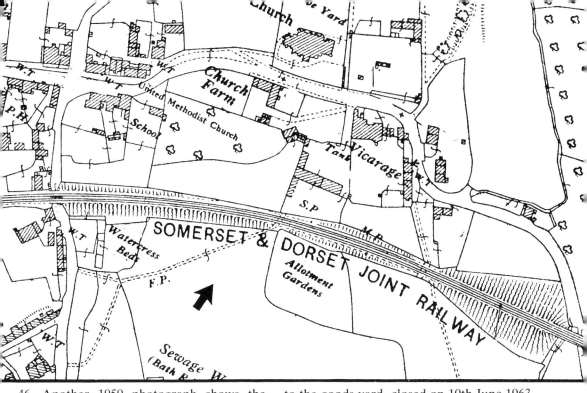

46. Another 1959 photograph shows the rodding tunnel in the up platform ramp and the adjacent hut which contained a ground frame controlling access to the sidings and the adjacent crossover. On the left is the gate to the goods yard, closed on 10th June 1963 to eventually become a public car park. The station building is now a private dwelling. (R.C. Riley)

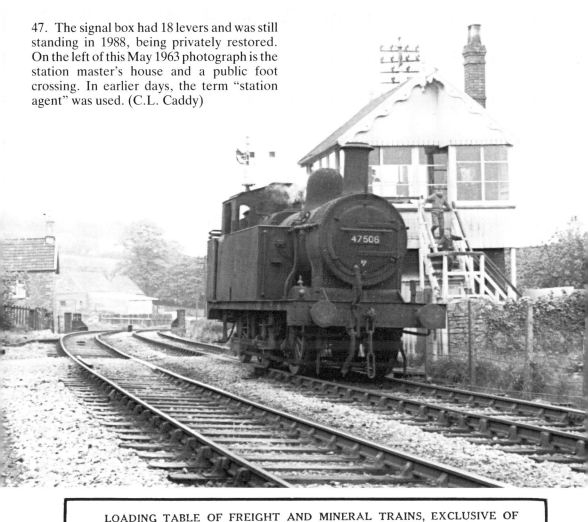

47. The signal box had 18 levers and was still standing in 1988, being privately restored. On the left of this May 1963 photograph is the station master's house and a public foot crossing. In earlier days, the term "station agent" was used. (C.L. Caddy)

LOADING TABLE OF FREIGHT AND MINERAL TRAINS, EXCLUSIVE OF BRAKE VANS.

	CLASS OF ENGINE.									
	1.		2		3.		4.		7.	
SECTION OF LINE (DOWN).	Minerals.	Maximum No. of Wagons.	Minerals.	Maximum No. of Wagons.	Minerals.	Maximum No. of Wagons.	Minerals.	Maximum No. of Wagons.	Minerals.	Maximum No. of Wagons.
Bath to Midford (**Banked**)	22	40	24	42	26	46	30	52	43	60
Bath to Midford (**Single load**)	11	20	13	23	15	26	17	35	17	40
Midford to Radstock	34	60	40	60	50	60	50	60	50	60
Radstock to Moorewood (**Banked**)	22	40	24	42	26	46	30	52	43	60
Radstock to Moorewood (**Single load**)	11	20	13	23	15	26	17	35	17	40
Moorewood to Binegar (**Banked**)	30	52	33	58	37	60	42	60	50	60
Moorewood to Binegar (**Single load**)	16	28	20	35	23	40	32	50	32	50
Binegar to Masbury (**Banked**)	26	46	26	46	26	46	30	52	50	60
Binegar to Masbury (**Single load**)	14	25	17	30	21	37	26	46	26	46
Masbury to Evercreech Junc.	26	46	26	46	26	46	30	52	43	60
SECTION OF LINE (UP).	1.		2.		3.		4.		7.	
Midford to Bath (**Single load**)	22	40	24	42	26	46	30	52	40	60
Radstock to Midford	34	60	40	60	40	60	40	60	40	60
Moorewood to Radstock (**Single load**)	26	46	26	46	26	46	30	52	43	66
Binegar to Moorewood (**Single load**)	30	52	36	60	43	66	50	66	50	66
Evercreech Junc. to Binegar (**Banked**)	22	40	24	42	26	46	30	52	43	66
Evercreech Junc. to Binegar (**Single load**)	11	20	13	23	15	26	17	35	17	40

1933 Appendix

SHOSCOMBE & SINGLE HILL HALT

48. The halt was constructed with SR concrete "harps and slabs" and came into use on 23rd September 1929. There were no shelters on the platforms but one was provided south of the line at the ticket office, which was staffed by two sisters for the entire 37 year life of the halt. Class 4 2–6–0 no.76027 speeds over the bridge towards Bournemouth on 3rd April 1965. (S.W. Baker)

1966 interim emergency service, prior to closure.

BATH GREEN PARK	06 45	08 15	16 25	18 10
Midford Halt	06 57	08 27	16 37	18 22
Wellow Halt	07 03	08 34	16 44	18 29
Shoscombe & Single Hill Halt	07 07	08 38	16 48	18 33
Radstock North	07 13	08 44	16 54	18 39
Midsomer Norton South	07 20	08 51	17 01	18 47
Chilcompton	07 28	08 59	17 09	18 55
Binegar	07 36	09 07	17 17	19 03
Masbury Halt	07 40	09 11	17 21	19 07
Shepton Mallet Charlton Road	07 50	09 18	17 29	19 15
Evercreech New	07 56	09 25	17 35	19 21
Evercreech Junction	08 00	09 29	17 38	19 24
Evercreech Junction	07 25	14 25	16 40	20 45
Evercreech New	07 31	14 31	16 46	20 51
Shepton Mallet Charlton Road	07 52	14 44	16 59	21 00
Masbury Halt	—	—	17 09	—
Binegar	08 08	14 58	17 15	V
Chilcompton	08 14	15 04	17 21	—
Midsomer Norton South	08 19	15 09	17 26	21 22
Radstock North	08 24	15 14	17 31	21 27
Shoscombe & Single Hill Halt	08 30	15 20	17 37	21 33
Wellow Halt	08 34	15 24	17 41	V
Midford Halt	08 40	15 30	17 47	V
BATH GREEN PARK	08 50	15 40	17 57	21 50

V — Calls to set down passengers on notice being given to the guard

WRITHLINGTON

With only about 500 parishioners, the village did not justify a station but colliery sidings were eventually provided on both sides of the main line. At Lower Writhlington, two shafts were sunk in 1829, the winding shaft being 10ft diameter and 1461ft deep. Steam winding was employed until 1966, the last in Somerset. Underground connections were made to Braysdown in 1953 and to Kilmersdon in 1959. Braysdown closed on 29th October 1959 and Lower Writhlington raised its last coal on 28th September 1973, the final coal train leaving on 16th October 1973.

49. The S&D main line is in the foreground and 0–4–2ST no.25A is standing on the line leading to the Writhlington Colliery sidings. This locomotive was in use from 1885 until 1929. The photograph was taken from the 2′6″ gauge incline to Braysdown Colliery. The building on the left houses the pumping engine, which kept the mine clear of water, and next to it is the winding engine house. The cable passes through the aperture in the gable end, to reach the headgear. The lean-to building houses the screens, under which two wagons await coal. The wagons on the extreme right belong to the Radstock coal factors, F. Bird & Co. Although previously published, this picture deserves careful examination in large form, as it is typical of the larger collieries of the area.
(Lens of Sutton)

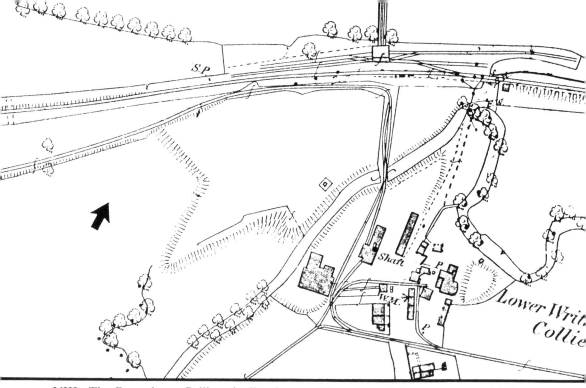

VIII. The Braysdown Colliery incline is at the top of this 1886 map and the SDJR single line from Radstock to Wellow runs from left to right. The line from Lower Writhlington Colliery to Ludlows Colliery and to the GWR (at Radstock) is seen on the left, following the original curved course of the canal. This route was abandoned in about 1886 when sidings were provided on the SDJR. Lower centre is a 2′8½″ gauge track, leading to Upper Writhlington Colliery and to the GWR (south of Radstock). Coal continued to be despatched by this route until 1940. Lower right, the line to Foxcote Colliery is shown.

50. The 0–6–0ST "Foxcote" was supplied new in 1890, by Hudswell Clarke (works no.369), to work the upper level around Foxcote Colliery, above Lower Writhlington. This it did until the pit closed in about 1920. (SDRT)

51. Writhlington Box was opened in July 1894 and replaced Foxcote Box, the unconventional signalling of which had been the cause of a head-on collision on 7th August 1876, resulting in twelve fatalities. The camera is on the site of Braysdown Colliery sidings (closed 13th April 1962) as the 3.20pm Bath to Templecombe runs past on 18th May 1963, headed by class 4 no.75072. (C.L. Caddy)

52. "Jinty" no.47276 shunts loaded wagons on 4th March 1966, while others wait under the hoppers for filling. After closure of the S&D main line, the down line was retained through Radstock North station to a new connection with the former GWR line. Lifted in 1975, it was the last part of the S&D main line to be removed. (S.C. Nash)

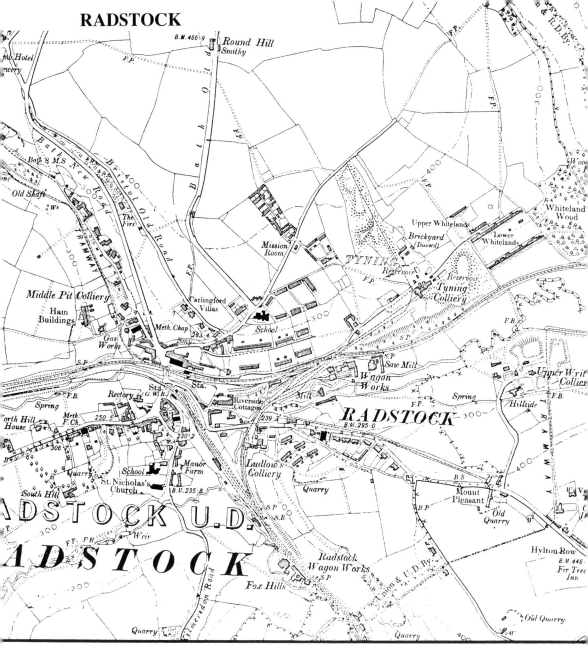

RADSTOCK

By 1800, Radstock was well established as a coal mining centre, the transport being by pack horse or cart. The GWR laid connections to many of the collieries soon after its arrival in 1854, leaving few for the SDR to serve exclusively when it opened 18 years later.

At the zenith of the railways, only about one third of the total coal output left the area by rail, and of this, only about 10 to 15% was carried by the S&D. Nevertheless, it is worth understanding something of the collieries that were connected to the route at various times.

Middle Pit was in use before 1800 and the shaft was enlarged to 10 x 1791 feet in 1884-86. It was connected to the S&D on 18th September 1882, the sidings remaining in use until 1955 to serve the adjacent gas works which dated from 1859.

Clandown Pit was served by a half mile extension of the line to Middle Pit. The line was in use between 1882 and 1922, the pit functioning from the 18th century until November 1929. Its shaft was 1437ft deep and only 6ft diameter.

Tyning Pit was in production from 1837 until 1909 but was not connected to the S&D. Its railways did, however, pass over the S&D and remained in use until 1954 for conveying waste to a tip.

The population rose from 2600 to 3400 in the last 30 years of the 19th century and it was labour shortage and the irregularity of the relatively thin coal seams (2 to 3ft) that brought about the demise of the industry.

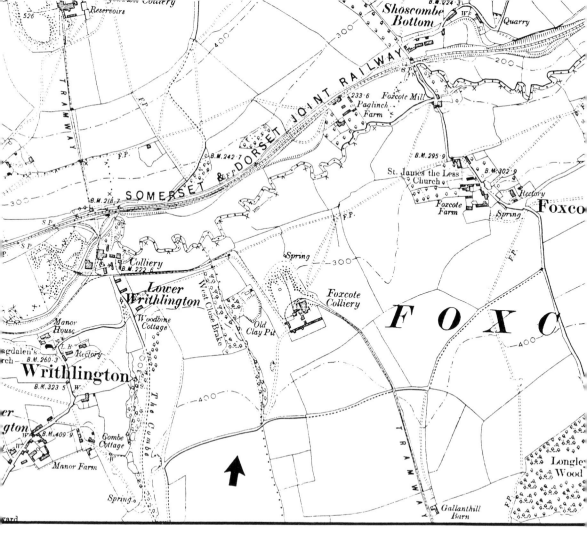

IX. The 6″ to 1 mile of 1904 gives the position of many of the collieries – Middle Pit, Ludlows, Tyning, Upper and Lower Writhlington, Foxcote and Braysdown. It also shows the GWR line to Frome at the bottom of the left page and the 2′8½″ gauge line from Foxcote Colliery to the Faulkland coal store at the bottom of the right hand page. Shoscombe & Single Hill Halt was later located by the 'Y' of *SOMERSET & DORSET JOINT RAILWAY*. Two wagon works are shown – the one close to the SDJR was initially only connected to the GWR and was the Wheeler & Gregory Wagon Works, which later became the British Wagon Company and finally Wagon Repairs Ltd, having expanded into the saw mills. These were originally operated by Edgerley Bros. whose raw material partly arrived via the S&D. It was later run by Mr. Temple Bourne, the main output being pit props and other timber for the collieries. At the bottom of the map is Radstock Wagon Works, which closed in 1988, the last train leaving on 29th June. The other wagon works closed in 1972.

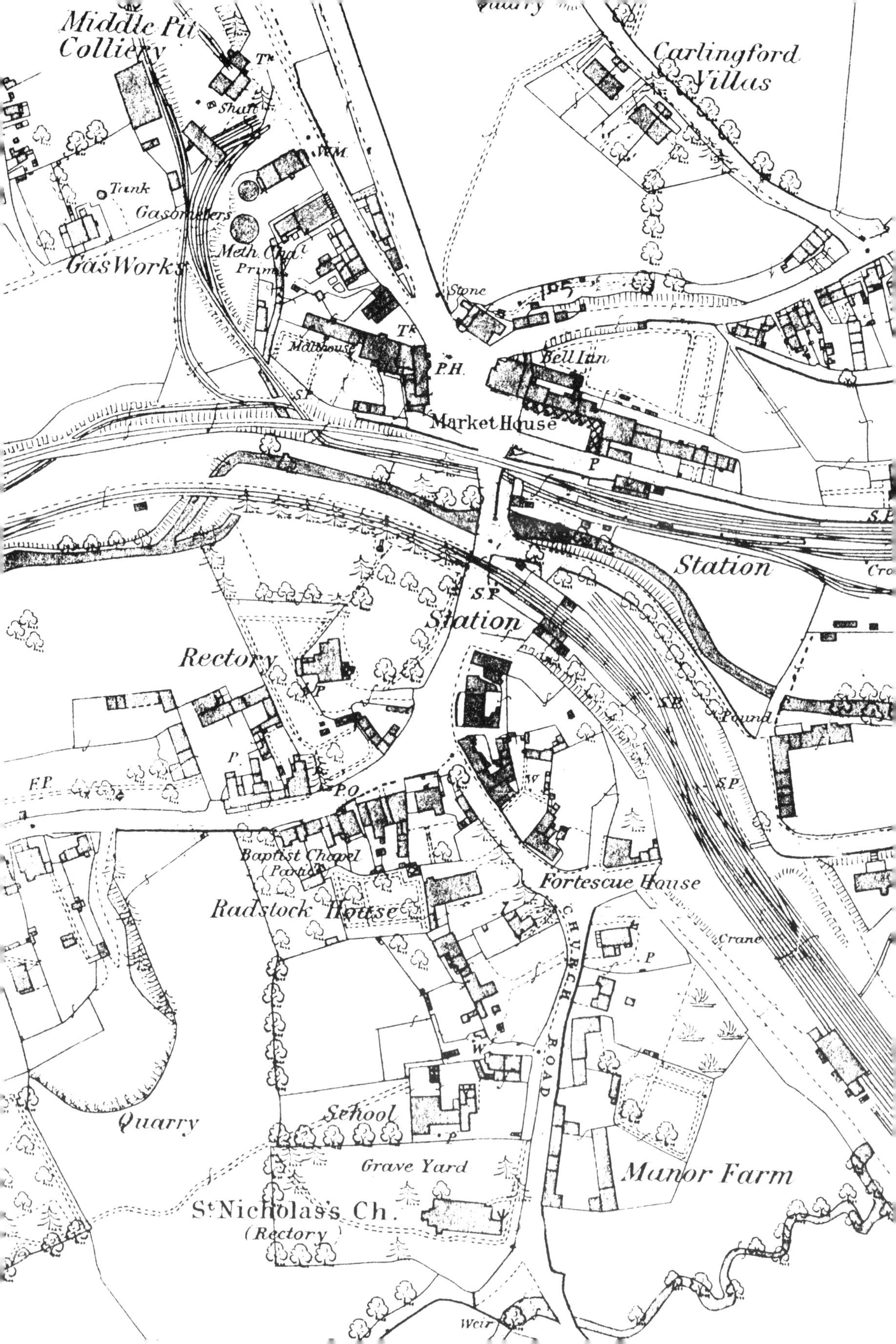

Middle Pit
Colliery

Carlingford
Villas

Tr

Shaft

Tank
Gasometers

Gas Works

Meth Chl
Prim.

Stone

Malthouse

Tr

P.H.

Bell Inn

Market House

P

SP

Station

Station

Rectory

SP

P

Pound

P

FP

P.O.

SP

Baptist Chapel
(Particular)

Fortescue House

Radstock House

Crane

CHURCH ROAD

P

Quarry

School

Grave Yard

Manor Farm

St Nicholas's Ch
(Rectory)

Weir

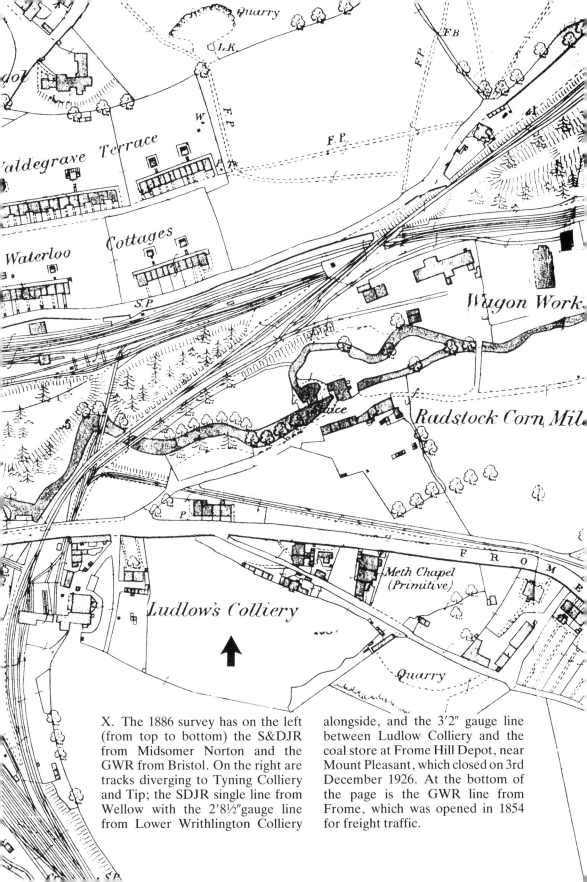

Quarry

L.K.

F.B.

F.P.

F.P.

W.

F.P.

Valdegrave Terrace

F.P.

Waterloo   Cottages

Wagon Work

S.P.

Radstock Corn Mil

P.

F R O M E

Meth Chapel
(Primitive)

Ludlow's Colliery

Quarry

X. The 1886 survey has on the left (from top to bottom) the S&DJR from Midsomer Norton and the GWR from Bristol. On the right are tracks diverging to Tyning Colliery and Tip; the SDJR single line from Wellow with the 2′8½″gauge line from Lower Writhlington Colliery alongside, and the 3′2″ gauge line between Ludlow Colliery and the coal store at Frome Hill Depot, near Mount Pleasant, which closed on 3rd December 1926. At the bottom of the page is the GWR line from Frome, which was opened in 1854 for freight traffic.

53. Ludlow's Colliery was started in about 1784 and continued production until 19th March 1954, when 117 men were yielding about 900 tons per week. In 1934, the workings were linked to Braysdown and in 1945 mechanical coal cutting was introduced, rare in Somerset. There were rail connections to both the S&D and the GWR.
(D. Cullum collection)

54. An up train passes over the level crossing, in about 1904, the chimney of the earlier signal box being visible beyond the footbridge. The water column at the end of the down platform and the inter-platform footbridge were lost in the 1950s.
(Lens of Sutton)

55. A short up train waits to depart behind no.18, which was later renumbered 15 and then 301. The structure on the left supports the middle of a public footbridge which passed over the main lines and others. (Lens of Sutton)

1910

SOMERSET and DORSET.—South Western and Midland.
Chief Eng., J. W. Jacomb Hood, Waterloo Station, London.   Res. Eng., E. R. Goche, Glastonbury.

56. A 1928 view from the public footbridge shows 4–4–0 no.77 hauling its down train between the stone-built engine shed and the wooden goods shed, which was similar to that used by the LSWR at Lyme Regis. On the left are Waterloo Cottages and an up freight train, which includes an LMS gunpowder van. (D. Cullum collection)

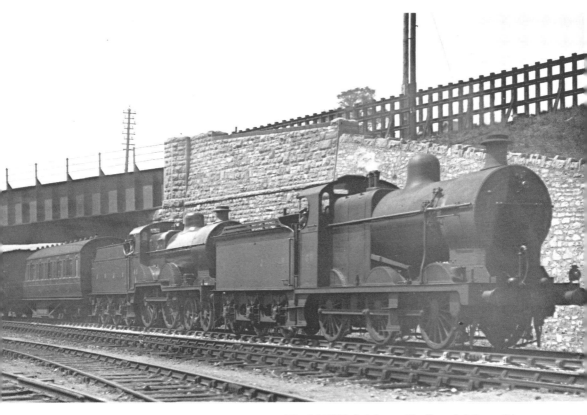

57. The lines of Tyning Colliery were carried over the Somerset Coal Canal's tramway by the stone arch, seen to the right of Radstock East Box, in this photograph from about 1894. The steel span on the left was erected when the main line to Bath was doubled, leaving a headroom of only 10′10″ on the siding under the arch. The map does not make it clear that standard and narrow gauge lines passed over these bridges on three-rail dual gauge track. The standard gauge line was removed in 1909 when Tyning Colliery closed, but the narrow gauge line to the tip or batch was retained. The restricting arch was demolished in 1960. (SDRT collection)

58. S&DJR 0-6-0 no. 60 pilots 4-4-0 no. 45 on 21st May 1929 and passes under Tyning bridge with a northbound express. The 0-6-0s were not suited to passenger trains - one undesirable feature being severe oscillation between engine and tender at speed. (H.C.Casserley)

59. The locomotives on view in May 1929 include 0–4–0ST no.26A and Sentinel 0–4–0 no.101, one of two acquired that year to replace 25A, 26A and 45A on local shunting duties. All were exceptionally squat, to clear Tyning Arch. Centre is class 3F 0–6–0 no.21 which at that time were ousting the 0–6–0STs (right) on banking duties. (H.C. Casserley)

60. Shedmasters were noted for their ability to improvise. This is the novel method of coaling locomotives in 1951. In its final years, the shed housed a diesel shunter for the coal trains and was demolished in 1979. (R.M. Casserley)

61. The peaks of the three Tyning waste tips are visible as no.34099 *Lynmouth* speeds past the goods yard on 27th July 1958 at 3.14pm, with the 10.10am from Sheffield to Bournemouth West. The East Box was renamed Radstock North 'A' Box in 1951 and was closed on 23rd August 1964. It had 17 levers. (R.C. Riley)

62. Looking west from "A" Box on 11th August 1962, we see (from left to right) the connection to Ludlow's Colliery (which once connected to the Frome line); the engine shed; the weighbridge hut; the whistle board (essential in the absence of a footbridge between the platforms) and the 9.55am Bournemouth West to Leeds, hauled by no. 34043 *Combe Martin*. (E.Wilmshurst)

64. Radstock North 'B' Box had a gate wheel but was closed at the cessation of passenger services after which the gates were opened by hand until the end of coal traffic in September 1973. The nearby box at the former GWR level crossing is now in use again at the Didcot Railway Centre. The Board of Trade required both railways to eliminate their level crossings in the town. The GWR ignored the order and the S&D provided this unbelievably inconvenient bridge under their line, seen in the centre of this May 1965 photograph. Having passed under the main lines, users were then confronted with a narrow gauge level crossing before climbing the ramp to the town – see the 1886 map. In the 1950s, increasing road traffic necessitated the provision of station staff, armed with red flags, to assist the signalman halt the cars which were often jammed for miles each side of the town on summer Saturdays. (H.C. Casserley)

63. "North" was added under the sign on 26th September 1949, the gradient post below indicating 1 in 300 down through the station and 1 in 55 up westwards, the beginning of a severe eight mile climb to Masbury. On the right of this February 1963 view is the square base of the former water column and the trackbed of the line that ran from the goods yard to the gas works and Middle Pit, passing under the road *and* the S&D main line. Originally narrow gauge, an additional rail was laid to standard gauge in 1881 to give mixed gauge. Upon doubling of the main line, a siding was laid direct from the up track to Middle Pit and Clandown Colliery, rendering the odd arrangement obsolete. The narrow gauge line was retained in use until the early 1930s, for the removal of waste from Middle Pit.

65. In 1970, the Somerset & Dorset Railway Trust leased part of Radstock shed and commenced restoration of class 7F no.53808, together with other S&D stock. This is the view on 12th May 1975, five months before transfer to Washford, on the West Somerset Railway, where an excellent S&D museum has been established. The locomotive began to haul pasengers on that line in September 1987, 23 years after being withdrawn. (SDRT/A. Vaughan)

67. About ½ mile west of the station, the S&D began to turn south and crossed the former GWR Radstock - Bristol single line. Class 2P no.40569 pilots class 9F no.92000 on the descent from Midsomer Norton with the 9.45am Bournemouth West to Manchester service on 22nd July 1961, the penultimate year of through trains to that city. Passenger services on the line to Bristol were withdrawn on 2nd November 1959 and freight traffic ceased in July 1968. (S.C. Nash)

66. Class 4 2–6–0 no.76006 is bound for Templecombe on 28th December 1965, as it climbs at 1 in 50 alongside the Frome - Bristol line. The connection came into use when the S&D closed, enabling coal trains from Writhlington to run to Bristol direct. Closure of the route in 1968 meant that coal trains had to reverse here and run via Frome and Westbury to reach the customers – Portishead Power Station and the Avonmouth Zinc Smelter. (E. Wilmshurst)

Norton Hill Colliery dated from about 1839, its original shaft being only 4′6″ diameter. In 1900-03, a new shaft was sunk, further north, being 13′6″ in diameter and 1500ft deep. The pit had one of the largest annual outputs in the district, e.g. 130,000 tons in 1939 and 149,000 tons in 1949, much of it leaving by rail. New sidings were laid in 1953 and the colliery was modernised then, and again in 1960, but to no avail; it closed on 11th February 1966 with the loss of 284 jobs.

68. Class 7F no.53810 has climbed two miles of the severe gradient from Radstock as it approaches Midsomer Norton with the morning Bath to Evercreech Junction freight on 26th June 1962. The line to Norton Hill Colliery, on the right, only climbed 17ft in its original ½ mile length so can be regarded as almost level in this view. (R.C. Riley)

Like Radstock, the town was once heavily dependent on coal for its income but had a population usually about 50% larger. It doubled from 4000 during the life of the S&D, the local industries expanding to include the manufacture of paper, footwear and timber buildings.

70. The suffix "& Welton" was added on 16th October 1898, this being replaced by "Upper" on 26th September 1949 and "South" on 25th September 1950. An up freight stands on the crossover on 3rd July 1961. (R.C. Riley)

MIDSOMER NORTON

69. Long skirts and milk churns cover much of the down platform as a down train arrives behind an SDJR 0–4–4T. The station was situated inconveniently high above the town, but closer than the GWR's. (Lens of Sutton)

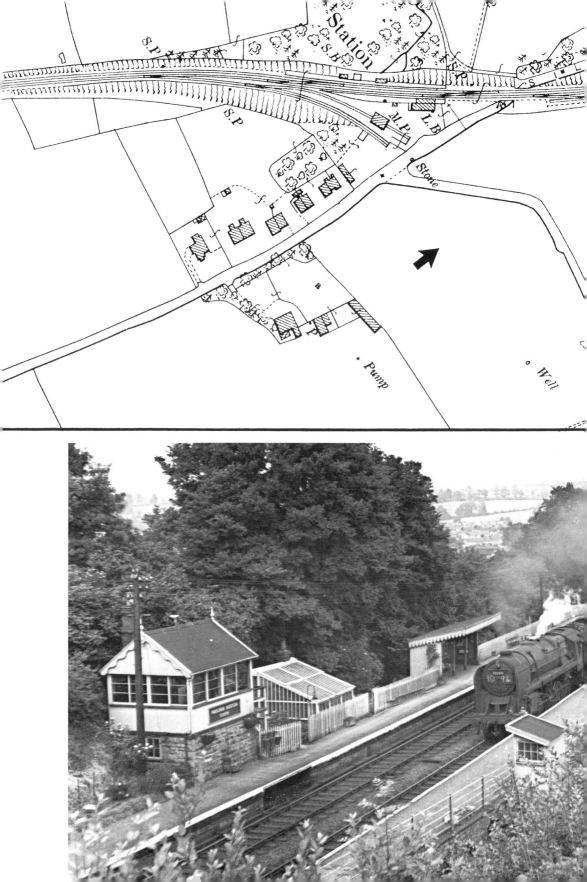

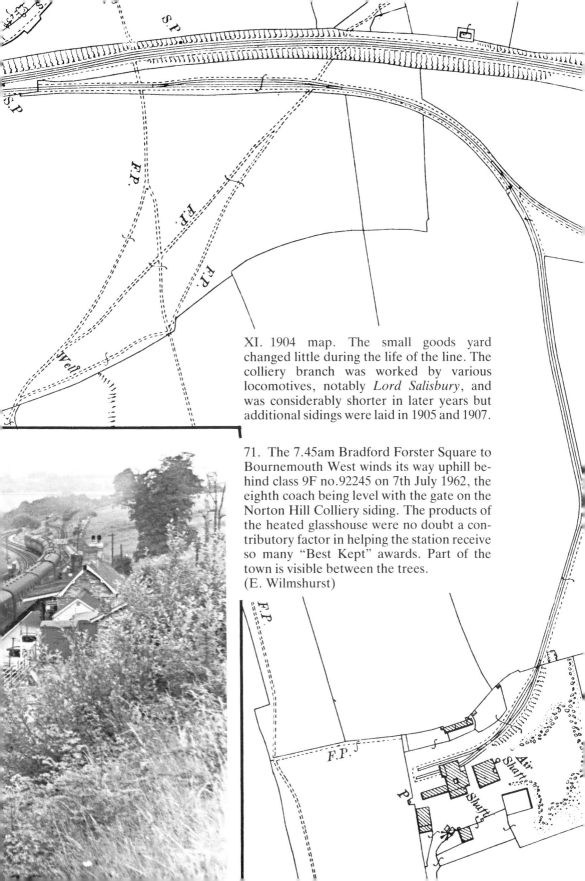

XI. 1904 map. The small goods yard changed little during the life of the line. The colliery branch was worked by various locomotives, notably *Lord Salisbury*, and was considerably shorter in later years but additional sidings were laid in 1905 and 1907.

71. The 7.45am Bradford Forster Square to Bournemouth West winds its way uphill behind class 9F no.92245 on 7th July 1962, the eighth coach being level with the gate on the Norton Hill Colliery siding. The products of the heated glasshouse were no doubt a contributory factor in helping the station receive so many "Best Kept" awards. Part of the town is visible between the trees.
(E. Wilmshurst)

72. Wagons stand in the small goods yard which remained open to the end of the line. The goods shed is obscured by the station, as a class 4 2–6–4T departs north on 3rd April 1965. Following more than 20 years of neglect after closure, the buildings were renovated as part of a community scheme. (S.W. Baker)

73. After a continuous climb at 1 in 53 for over a mile after leaving Midsomer Norton, class 2P no.40652 and class 5 no.73019 clear the 66yd Chilcompton Tunnel on 5th September 1959. Present day charter airline passengers suffer inconvenient departure times – nothing changes in pursuit of a holiday – travellers from Bradford boarded this train at 7.40am! (R.C. Riley)

CHILCOMPTON

74. No.45 rounds the last curve into the down platform in 1909, the house being visible in the background of the next picture. With an altitude of 600ft above sea level, snow can be a problem here. Downside School generated considerable traffic at this station, notably with special trains at each end of every term. (D. Cullum collection)

The number of inhabitants changed little during the life of the line (600-800), the nearby New Rock Colliery employing about 200 men. It started in 1819, with a 4'6" winding shaft, and latterly produced about 200 tons per day, in two shifts, closing on 28th September 1968. The southern boundary of the Somerset Coalfield is in this area.

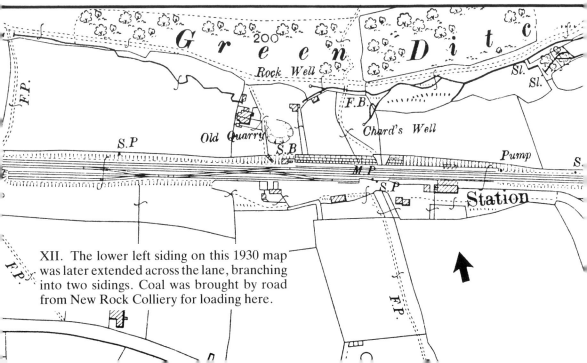

XII. The lower left siding on this 1930 map was later extended across the lane, branching into two sidings. Coal was brought by road from New Rock Colliery for loading here.

75. The usual offices were provided on the down side, close to the approach road. Bridge no.53, which accommodated a footpath, accounts for the kink in the up platform. As at Midsomer Norton, the 1 in 50 gradient eased to 1 in 300 through the station, the change being evident in the distance. (C.L. Caddy)

76. Turning nearly 180°, we see the goods shed, 5-ton crane, well lagged water column and 13-lever signal box, on 18th May 1963. All were closed on 11th April 1965. Hereabouts, the line is on the south side of the valley of the Rover Somer, where calamine (zinc carbonate) was once quarried. (C.L. Caddy)

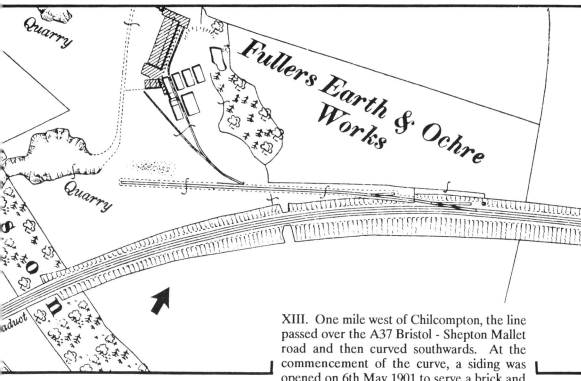

77. In 1914, Moorewood sidings were opened on the south side of the main line to load coal from Moorewood Colliery and also stone, which was conveyed by aerial ropeway from Clement Dalley's Quarry, until 1930. Class 2P no.40700 and "West Country" no.34041 *Wilton* pass with the 12.20pm Bournemouth West to Nottingham, on 15th July 1961. The sidings were retained for storage of empty wagons for the Emborough Quarry. (S.C. Nash)

XIII. One mile west of Chilcompton, the line passed over the A37 Bristol - Shepton Mallet road and then curved southwards. At the commencement of the curve, a siding was opened on 6th May 1901 to serve a brick and tile works, also the premises of the Somerset Fullers Earth and Ochre Co. Ltd. at Old Down. Both yellow and red ochre were produced here briefly, for the paint and manufacturing industries, but had probably ceased by 1903 when this survey was made. After the failure of the ochre enterprise, the quarry was acquired by the Emborough Stone Co. Ltd. who also started quarrying south of the line, laying a tramway under Nettlebridge Viaduct, lower left.

Moorewood Colliery was started in the 1860s and became fully operational in 1913. It had a 9ft diameter shaft, only 888ft deep, coal being conveyed on a 2ft gauge railway to the S&D sidings. This line included a lengthy incline and was operational until 1925. Road transport was used until the colliery closed on 7th December 1932.

78. The Old Down ground frame was abolished when the 19-lever Moorewood Box was opened in 1914. It was on the up side with Emborough sidings to the west and Moorewood to the east. The box is obscured by the rear of the train in picture no. 77. It closed on 5th July 1965, the sidings having been closed on 9th December 1964. (C.L.Caddy)

80. LMS no.628 stands in the up platform on 23rd July 1937, coupled to a flat wagon carrying a "suitcase of industry", as the publicity sometimes described a container. The final climb of 1 in 63 to Masbury commences by the crossover in the distance.
(H.C. Casserley)

BINEGAR

79. The well tended flower beds in the foreground typify the pride taken by S&D railwaymen in the appearance of their stations. Barrels by the "Gents" are a reminder that the Oakhill Brewery operated a 3ft gauge railway to the station, between 1904 and 1921. The limekiln is in the distance. (Lens of Sutton)

The village is a little over 700ft above sea level and had less than 300 inhabitants in the 19th century. In 1903, sidings were brought into use to serve Read & Sons Mendip Stone Works. This included a lime kiln and stone crushing plant. It was connected to another quarry at Gurney Slade, by aerial ropeway.

81. Class 7F no.53802 struggles past the loading dock on 14th August 1954, the train being banked by class 3F no.47466 at the rear. The station master's house on the right was occupied by Mr. Norman Down from 1944 until his death in 1988. The goods yard closed on 10th June 1963. (S.C. Nash)

XIV. The station layout changed considerably from the 1903 arrangement, seen here. Two sidings were added. The siding on the right eventually fanned out into three tracks

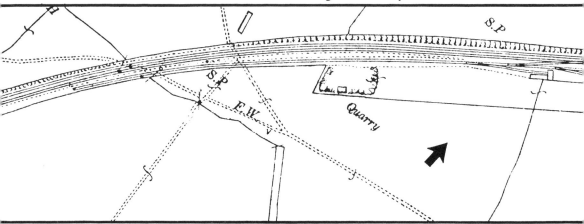

in Read & Sons' quarry. Two goods sheds are shown, the larger one containing a one-ton crane.

82. The apparatus to the right of the foot crossing held the banking engine key which was picked up to authorise the driver to return "wrong road", after reaching the summit one mile south. The apparatus and the banking engine key are now in the SDRT Museum. The stone crushing plant, in the background, was latterly operated by Roads Reconstruction (1934) Ltd. (Lens of Sutton)

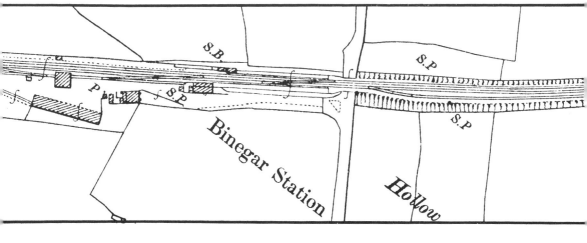

83. "Jinty" class 3Fs were commonly used for banking down freight trains from Radstock. No.47316 was on duty on 3rd July 1961 and returns on the up line, having used the crossover south of the station. (R.C. Riley)

85. Many photographs were taken from the brake van of down freight trains as the banking engine left the train at Masbury Summit, 811ft above sea level. This one is unusual in that the summit had not been reached. It was south of the B3135 Cheddar - Oakhill road bridge, the abutment of which is visible. The guard uncoupled the locomotive using a hook, which was then re-hung on the smokebox door. Masbury is locally spelt Maesbury and pronounced Marsbury. (R.C. Riley)

USE OF LEVEL CROSSINGS BY THE MENDIP HUNT.

An agreement has been entered into between the Somerset & Dorset Joint Line and the Master of the Mendip Fox Hounds, whereby the Master has been supplied with keys of the undermentioned level crossings for the purpose of allowing the Master and all other persons authorised by him to directly cross the railway, either while actually hunting or returning from hunting with the fox hounds.

Mileage.		Stations between
m.	ch.	
12	50	... Midsomer Norton and Chilcompton.
14	12¾	... Chilcompton and Binegar.
14	41	... Chilcompton and Binegar.
19	25	... Masbury and Shepton Mallet.
20	40½	... Masbury and Shepton Mallet.

It will be noted authority is only given to allow the " Hunt " to cross directly over the railway and under no circumstances must any member of the " Hunt," either on horse-back, vehicle or foot travel along the railway or the Committee's land adjacent thereto.

Trainmen to particularly note this agreement and keep a sharp look-out.

1933

◄

84. The platform surface was crumbling from frequent frosts at this altitude and not from the feet of hordes of passengers. In the final years of operation, one train terminated here – the 6.05pm from Bath. The two or three coaches were often "Jinty" hauled. (C.L. Caddy)

MASBURY HALT

86. Nearly ½ mile south of the summit, the small station became a halt when staffing ceased on 26th September 1938. Looking south in July 1937, we see that the station house, beyond the signal box, was much larger than the station building. The goods yard, on the right, was closed on 10th June 1963, whereas the sidings at the Mendipadam Works opposite were lifted in 1959, having opened in 1928. (H.C. Casserley)

WINSOR HILL

88. Before passing through the tunnel 1½ miles south of Masbury, sidings were to be seen on the right for Hamwood Quarry. These were opened in 1893, shortly before this photograph was taken, and were little used after WWII. On the left are the sidings for Winsor Hill Quarry which also produced large quantities of crushed limestone. A single siding was provided here as early as 1875, this view dating from about 1893. (SDRT collection)

87. There had been considerable additional traffic during WWII when a USA Army camp was opened nearby. Steps were provided from the down platform to the white gate on the right. The signal box was closed on 1st July 1964; the house remains occupied although the station stands derelict. (Lens of Sutton)

89. The view north in September 1964 includes the Hamwood Quarry stone crushing plant and a fine panorama of the Mendip Plateau. The all-stone 16-lever signal box closed on 3rd August 1948. (S.W. Baker)

90. Class 9F no. 92245 hauls the 9.25am Bournemouth West to Liverpool Lime Street through the 126yd-long up tunnel on 7th July 1962. The down bore was the oldest and 239yds in length. The headings of the new bore met at 6.00am on 2nd July 1892. (E.Wilmshurst)

91. South of Winsor Hill tunnels, catch points were provided on the up line on the 1 in 50 gradient, to de-rail any runaway vehicles. A class 7F heads the Cleethorpes to Exmouth holidaymakers' train on 11th August 1962 and is about to pass the site of Downside Quarry which opened on 25th October 1900 and remained in use for about 40 years. This locomotive was previously seen in Radstock shed and is now to be found on the West Somerset Railway. (R.C. Riley)

92. Half a mile south of Winsor Hill and ½ mile north of Shepton Mallet town centre, the line passed over Bath Road on a 118yd-long viaduct. It had been widened in 1892 on the up side and it was this part which collapsed at 10.55pm on 1st February 1946. The up side had been deemed unsafe three days earlier and single working introduced, which remained in force until 1st August 1946. (SDRT collection)

93. A further ½ mile south, the route crossed another but longer (317yd) viaduct. The 27 arches were unusual in being segmental and not semi-circular. This design resulted in large lateral thrusts and required the 9th and 18th piers to be thicker. Every third pier was buttressed on the outside of the curve to resist the lateral forces of fast trains. (S.C. Nash)

94. A falling gradient of 1 in 55 and 1 in 130 changes to a rising one of 1 in 66 on Charlton viaduct. The 9.40am Sheffield to Bournemouth West is rising at 1 in 55 towards Shepton Mallet station on 20th August 1955, headed by class 2P no.40698 piloting class 5 no.73050. (S.C. Nash)

SHEPTON MALLET

An attractive market town, it retains many buildings from the 17th and 18th century and a much older market cross. An important commercial centre for a wide district, the town's population remained steady at 5000 to 5500 during the life of the line.

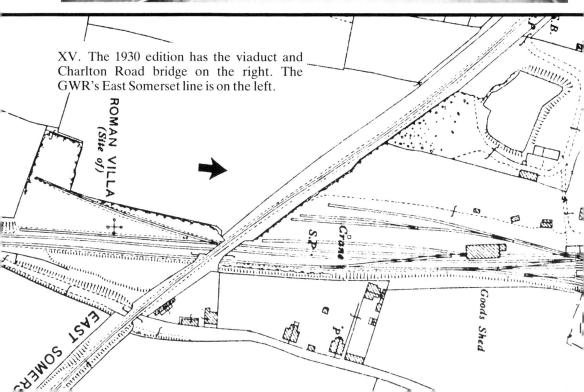

XV. The 1930 edition has the viaduct and Charlton Road bridge on the right. The GWR's East Somerset line is on the left.

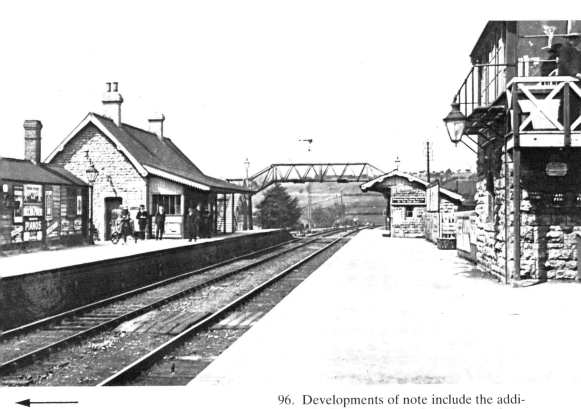

95. A pre-1900 northward view includes Charlton Viaduct, which was later obscured by trees, and emphasises its low level relative to the station. Other features of interest are the original footbridge and lack of parcels office. (SDRT collection)

96. Developments of note include the addition of a balcony to the signal box, replacement of the footbridge and the erection of a wooden parcels office, ideal for the reception of enamelled advertisement panels. (Lens of Sutton)

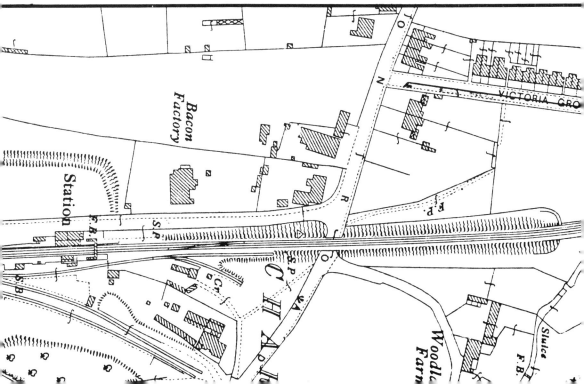

97. A southward view from the footbridge on 14th August 1954 shows class 2P no.40696 arriving with the 9.10am from Templecombe and the goods shed, near the rear coach. Part of the disused Charlton Lias Limeworks is visible. (S.C. Nash)

98. Class 7F no. 53805 waits to recommence its journey south with the 12.35pm Bath to Evercreech Junction while a coach, probably a cripple, stands by the cattle dock on 29th September 1959. (R.C.Riley)

99. The extent of the cattle dock and the chimney of the bacon factory are evident in this view from 11th November 1961. The now much admired class 7F, no.53808, runs over the down yard catch point, the siding on the right being used for cattle wagon cleaning and the one adjacent to it, for stone loading. (P. Hay)

100. Cleethorpes to Exmouth was an unusual coast to coast service operated on summer Saturdays. Class 4 no.75009 is piloting class 7F no.53810 on this train on 18th August 1962. The photographer was standing close to the 5-ton goods crane.
(S.C. Nash)

101. Most down freight trains stopped for water here after the arduous climb from Radstock. Class 7F no.53809 was pictured on 6th October 1962 and is now usually to be found at the Midland Railway Centre near Ripley in Derbyshire. The down sidings on the right once served the SDJR signal works and also a quarry for track ballast.
(R.C. Riley)

102. The capacious water tank is in the down yard, the longest siding of which terminates by the tree. The suffix "Charlton Road" was added in October 1883 to distinguish it from the GWR "Town Street", later "High Street", station. The signal box had 26 levers and remained open to the end of traffic.
(E. Wilmshurst)

103. A telegraph pole hides the signal post in this 1965 view of the spartan nameless exterior. Charlton Viaduct is visible beyond the station approach, which is illuminated by one gas lamp. (R.M. Casserley)

←

104. Closure was inevitable as passengers voted with their feet, but bitterness was intense regarding the manner in which it was executed. Dereliction was to be found everywhere for more than two years. This is the scene during track lifting on 6th April 1968. (S.W. Baker)

→

106. Class 4F no.44424 and "West Country" class no.34028 Eddystone speed south with clear exhausts and approach one of the signals built by the SR from two redundant running rails. The goods yard closed on 10th July 1963, but the siding to the left of the wagons had been lifted in 1955. (D. Fereday Glenn)

105. The brick arch spanned the original main line and is crossed by a 45XX class 2-6-2T on 5th October 1951, proceeding from Frome to Wells. Passenger services at Shepton Mallet High Street ceased on 9th September 1963 and goods on 13th July 1964. Behind class 7F no.53802 is the southern part of the up yard, which had once been the scene of quarrying for railway ballast. (S.C. Nash)

107. 1½ miles south of Shepton Mallet, near Prestleigh, another elegant viaduct is still to be found, a monument to a much loved railway. Railway enthusiasts filled this LCGB special on 30th September 1962, which is seen climbing the 1 in 50 incline north, behind class 7F no.53808 which is still giving pleasure to travellers on the West Somerset Railway. (S.C. Nash)

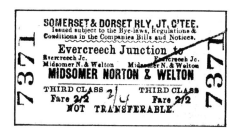

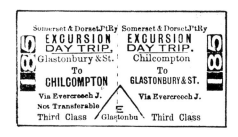

109. The signal box had 20 levers and is displaying the oval plate which was turned through 90° to indicate to the travelling linesman that his services were required. The original box was destroyed by fire in 1918. (D. Cullum collection)

EVERCREECH NEW

Situated on the southern slope of the Mendips, the substantial village was once noted for its horse and cattle markets. Containing many charming limestone dwellings of considerable age, the population was around 1200 while the railway was in operation.

108. An unusual evening view during shunting operations in 1932 shows the weighing machine on the platform and the cheese store, beyond the lamp post on the right. The general goods shed and the Mendips are in the distance. (D. Cullum collection)

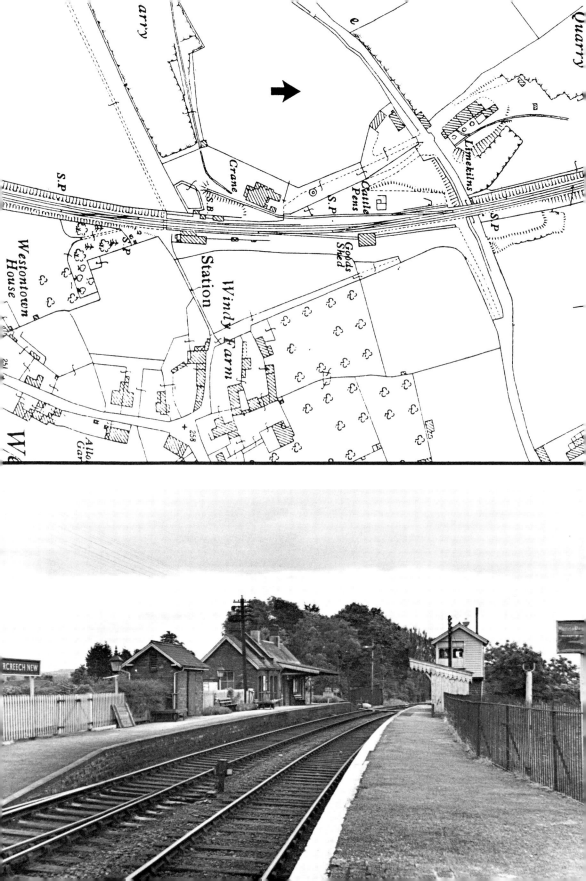

XVI. This 1930 edition shows two quarries, both with narrow guage railways, only the one on the right being shown on the 1903 survey. The cattle pens were demolished in 1930.

111. The siding to Evercreech Lime & Stone Co. passed between the signal box and the company's massive lime kiln. This July 1962 view shows that the goods yard was still busy and that a bell was provided by the foot crossing. The 1933 Appendix shows that it was then operated by treadles near the distant signals and could be started or stopped by the signalman. (R.C. Riley)

110. Looking south in 1962, we see a peeling notice on the right which once ordered BR locomotives not to pass. It is located by the gate to the limeworks siding. The goods yard and signal box closed on 11th October 1964. (E. Wilmshurst)

112. Class 2P no.40697 leaves the final curve of the Bath extension as it approaches Evercreech Junction on 11th September 1957. Curves were numerous on the 25-mile route owing to the geography and six miles of former canal route. (P. Hay)

113. Class 7F no.53803 leaves the junction on the same day with 20 empty mineral wagons, the Burnham branch being on the other side of the field. These locomotives seldom ran tender first after 1934, when adequate turntables were provided. Until about 1920, the first six were fitted with tender cabs. (P. Hay)

EVERCREECH JUNCTION

114. The space between the platforms was greater here than at other stations on the route, as the tracks of the Somerset Central Railway were initially broad gauge. This view towards the junction is thought to date from the 1890s. (National Railway Museum)

0625

S. & D. Rly. Jt. C'tee.
Issued subject to the Bye-laws,
Regulations & Conditions in the
Companies Bills and Notices.

Cheap as advertised

Shepton Mallet,
Charlton Road to
EVERCREECH JC.
Third Class
NOT TRANSFERABLE
- - - - - - - - - - - - -
S. & D. Ry Jt C'tee
CHEAP DAY

Evercreech Jc.
Shepton Mallet
Charlton Rd.
Evercreech Jc. to
SHEPTON MALLET,
CHARLTON ROAD
Third Class.

0626

641
SOM. & D. J'T RLY. RETURN
HALF DAY EXC'N.
BURNHAM to
BINEGAR
Via Evercreech Junc.
THIRD CLASS.
(See over)

SOM. & D. J'T RLY.
HALF DAY EXC
BINEGAR to
BURNHAM
Via Evercreech Junc.
THIRD CLASS.
641

Other views and a map of this station are included in the companion albums *Bournemouth to Evercreech Junction* **and** *Burnham to Evercreech Junction.*

115. One of the first railway enthusiasts excursions over the S&D was organised by Ian Allan Ltd, on 25th April 1954, when such trips were a rarity. So was the appearance of a "Schools" class. No.30392 *Blundells* was piloting 2P class no.40601.
(D. Cullum collection)

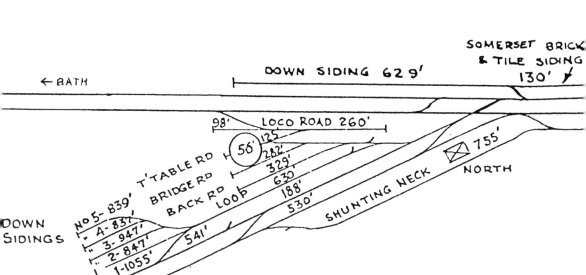

116. The station was inconveniently situated on a gradient (1 in 105), as can be seen by relating to the level sidings of New Yard in the distance in this 1958 picture. The station buildings survive today, unlike the two to the north. The goods yard closed on 29th November 1965, later than most.
(S.W. Baker)

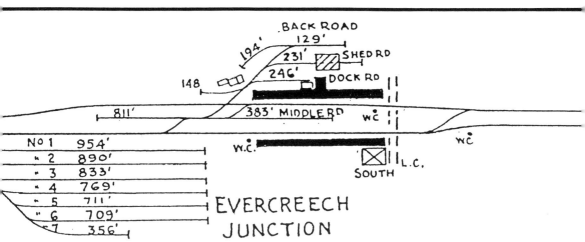

BACK ROAD

129'

194'   231'   SHED RD

148   246'   DOCK RD

811'   383' MIDDLE RD   WC

N° 1   954'
" 2   890'
" 3   833'
" 4   769'
" 5   711'
" 6   709'
" 7   356'

W.C.

WC

L.C.
SOUTH

EVERCREECH
JUNCTION

XVII. Control diagrams were first issued during WWII and were of great value as all loop and siding lengths were shown (or shewn, as it was then spelled).

117. Most southbound freights stopped after passing over the junction points and waited for the backing signal to be lowered, before reversing into the down yard. Class 7F no.53809 is undertaking this operation on 6th July 1957, under the control of the 32-lever North Box, on the left. The box was damaged by fire on 5th March 1966. (R.C. Riley)

118. Class 7F no.53810 arrives with the 11.00am freight from Bath on 26th June 1962 and passes the unusual buffer stops on the middle road. These are fitted with a three-link coupling to secure vehicles on the gradient down to the station. The siding was usually used by the Burnham branch train between trips and by banking engines awaiting up trains. (R.C. Riley)

119. Gloomy skies added to the sadness of the occasion on 5th March 1966 as the LCGB farewell tour departed north. It was not the last train, as final specials ran on the next day. The locomotives are class 2 2–6–2Ts nos.41307 and 41249. (J.H. Bird)

120. A final glimpse over the level crossing gates, such as would have been shared by countless frustrated road users, reminds us of the antiquated charm that attracted railway admirers in profusion to this splendid scenic route. (Lens of Sutton)

ACKNOWLEDGMENTS

We are very grateful for the help received from many of the photographers mentioned in the captions and also from Dr.P.Cattermole (Museum Curator of the Somerset and Dorset Railway Trust), R.Dagger, S.Ehrlicher, J.Fairman, C.Handley, D.Knapman, R.Resch, E.Staff, N.Stanyon, J.Wilkerson, T.Wright and our wives. Tickets have been kindly provided by G.Croughton and N.Langridge.

We are indebted to I.G.Morris and C.Osment for information incorporated in this revision.